my first
GARDENING
BOOK

35 easy and fun projects
for budding gardeners

CICO **kidz**

Published in 2016 by CICO Kidz
An imprint of Ryland Peters & Small Ltd
20–21 Jockey's Fields   341 E 116th St
London WC1R 4BW   New York, NY 10029

www.rylandpeters.com

10 9 8 7 6 5 4 3 2 1

A CIP catalog record for this book is available from
the Library of Congress and the British Library.

ISBN: 978 1 78249 333 4

Printed in China

Series consultant: Susan Akass
Editor: Clare Sayer
Designer: Barbara Zuniga
Illustrator: Hannah George

In-house editor: Dawn Bates
In-house designer: Fahema Khanam
Art director: Sally Powell
Production manager: Gordana Simakovic
Publishing manager: Penny Craig
Publisher: Cindy Richards

For photography credits, see page 112

Contents

Introduction

Do you enjoy being outside in the fresh air? Do you like nature and plants and seeing things grow? Do you like to have something of your own to look after? If the answer to these questions is "Yes!", then you need to begin some gardening!

My First Gardening Book will get you going with fun projects for every sort of garden, from a tiny teacup to a big backyard.

This book is divided into four chapters. Chapter 1 tells you all you need to know to begin gardening —what tools to get, how to prepare a plot, how to plant seeds, how to plant in containers, and how to look after your plants once they are growing. Chapter 2 has lots of different gardening projects, some for outside plots and some for growing in containers. The plants you grow in these projects may grow huge like sunflowers, or stay very small, like the plants you can grow in an eggshell! Chapter 3 tells you different ways to decorate your garden with exciting ideas like an ice mobile for frosty days or a mini scarecrow to scare away the birds. Finally, Chapter 4 has all sorts of unusual garden craft ideas to keep you busy and happy on rainy days when you can't be outside.

To help you know where to begin, we have graded all the projects with one, two, or three smiley faces. Level 1 projects are easy and you will quickly make something lovely. Level 2 projects need a few more skills and take longer, so you will need a bit more patience. Level 3 projects are real gardening projects and gardens don't grow overnight! These will keep you busy for weeks or months, but you will create something wonderful and learn lots of new gardening skills.

So what are you waiting for—pull on those boots and get gardening!

Project levels

Level 1
These are easy projects with quick results.

Level 2
These projects need a few more skills and will take longer to complete.

Level 3
These projects will keep you busy for weeks or months and teach you lots of new skills.

chapter 1
Getting Started

Garden Tools

If you don't have a plot in the garden but are just growing your plants in containers, a trowel and a watering can are all you will need. However, if you have a plot of ground for your gardening you will need some other tools. You could use a standard adult hand fork and trowel but other adult tools—garden spade, garden fork, rake, and hoe—will be too big for you and difficult and also dangerous to use. You will need to get tools designed for children, but don't get baby ones! You need proper, good-quality tools in slightly smaller sizes (see Suppliers on page 111).

Large tools

• **Garden spade**
A spade is used to prepare the soil by digging it up and turning it over.

• **Garden fork**
A garden fork can be used in the same way as a spade if the soil is sticky and heavy or full of stones. You can also use it for breaking up big clods of soil or for tossing on manure or compost. Another use is for digging out plants, either weeds you want to get rid of or plants you want to move.

! SAFETY FIRST

When you are not using your fork, push it upright into the ground so no one can stand on the sharp prongs.

! SAFETY FIRST

When you are not using your rake, lie it down with the teeth pushed into the soil. If it is the other way up and you step on it, the handle shoots up and whacks you in the face!

• **Rake**
A rake is used to break up the soil into a fine tilth (small pieces with no big lumps or stones.) It is especially important to do this when planting tiny seeds.

• **Hoe**
A hoe is used for cutting down weeds between your plants.

• **Wheelbarrow**
A wheelbarrow is really useful for carrying all your equipment. It can also be used to help move soil or compost or for carrying your vegetables when you have dug them up.

Hand tools

• Trowel
When planting a new plant in your garden, use
a trowel to dig a hole for it and then use it again to
cover its roots with soil. A trowel is also useful for
scooping potting mix (compost) out of a sack.

• Hand fork
A hand fork is useful for digging up weeds and for
loosening soil in small spaces around your plants.

• Watering can
No plants or seeds will grow without water. Water
them using a can with a fine rose (this is on the end
of the spout) so that the water doesn't disturb the
soil. Water is heavy so have a smallish can that you
can carry when full.

Other useful equipment

• **Bucket**
Have a bucket handy when you are weeding your plot because you need somewhere to put the weeds you pull out. You can also use it when collecting your vegetables.

• **Scissors and string or plastic-coated wire**
These are needed for when you are tying plants to canes.

• **Seed labels and pencil**
Popsicle (lolly) sticks make good labels for the seeds you have just planted.

What to wear

• Gardening gloves—buy special children's gardening gloves and always wear them when you are digging or using manure, to stop you picking up nasty illnesses.

• Rain (wellington) boots or sturdy shoes to keep your feet clean and dry and to protect them from sharp stones.

• A sun hat and sun cream for sunny days.

• Old clothes that you don't mind getting muddy!

! SAFETY TIP

It is VERY IMPORTANT that you wash your hands thoroughly with soap and water every time you come inside after gardening.

Preparing Your Patch

Before you can begin to grow any plants in your garden, you need to prepare your patch of soil. Some gardeners will do this in the fall (autumn) but then you have to wait a long time before you plant anything, so it is fine to begin in the spring.

1 Ask an adult to let you have an open, sunny plot of garden roughly 40 x 40 in (1 x 1 meter). Ask to have one close to a faucet (tap) or water butt so you won't have to carry water too far to water your plants.

2 Ask an adult to help you to dig your garden the first time because digging new ground is hard work. However, if it has been dug once you might want to do a better job yourself, using your own spade or fork.

Digging your patch will loosen the soil so the plants can grow easily and will take out any weeds. It is also a chance to add some compost or manure (see page 14) to make your plants grow healthy and strong. Digging is fun and will give you good muscles.

• Hold the spade or fork vertical, holding the handle with both hands. Put one foot on the blade and push it into the soil, putting all your weight on your foot.

• Lower the handle down toward you, pushing hard. This will lever up a clod of soil.

• Bend your knees and then lift the soil and drop it in front of the place where it came from, turning it over as you drop it. This will leave a hole in front of you and a pile of soil behind it.

• Pick out any weeds or stones that you have brought to the surface.

• Work in a line across your patch digging a trench, then step back and start another trench behind the first. The soil you dig this time will drop into the trench you made last time.

Digging tips

• You could add some manure to the trench at the end of each row, which will then get covered up as you dig the next row.

• If your soil is sticky and heavy, you could use your fork for digging instead.

• Use your wheelbarrow to move the soil from the first pile back into your last trench.

3 Next you need to work the soil into a fine tilth, which means it is fine and crumbly with no lumps. Use a rake to do this, pushing and pulling the rake backward and forward, combing it through the soil. You could also bash down on bigger lumps to break them up. Take out any stones and weeds you rake up. Then use the rake to level the soil so it is all flat.

4 Next, wearing your boots, walk up and down, heel to toe, all over the soil pressing it down gently.

5 When your patch is beautifully prepared, mark the edges with pebbles, shells, bricks, or lengths of log. You could even make a fun sign painted with your name.

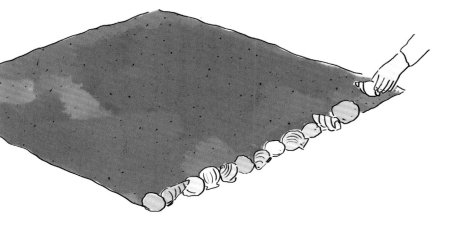

Planting Seeds Outside

Planting (or sowing) from seed is the most exciting part of gardening. Some seeds (carrots, calendula, beets/beetroot, chard) are best sown straight into the soil. Check on the seed packet when you should sow them.

1 Once you have prepared your soil, plan which seeds you are going to plant and where you are going to plant them. Check where shadows fall—your plants need lots of sun. Tall plants should be planted where they won't shade smaller ones and remember to space the rows out—plants grow quickly!

2 Check the seed packet to see how deep the seeds should be planted. For small seeds it needs to be about ½ in (1 cm) deep. Bigger seeds, such as dwarf beans, need to be planted deeper.

3 Lay a garden cane flat on the soil where you want your row of seeds to grow. Use the edge of a hoe or a trowel to dig a groove for your seeds, using the cane like a ruler. Mark the row: write the name of the seed you are going to plant on a seed label—popsicle (lolly) sticks are good for this—and push it into the soil at one end of the row. Push a stick into the soil at the other end.

4 Tip some seeds into your hand and sprinkle them thinly along the groove. With larger seeds place them in one by one, spacing them apart (check the packet for spacing).

5 Use a rake, hoe, or even your hands to cover the seeds with fine, lump-free soil and gently press down the soil with your hands.

6 Water your seeds using a watering can with a fine rose so that you don't wash the seeds away. Check every day to see if the seedlings have appeared and if they need watering. Some tiny ones, such as arugula (rocket), appear a few days after you have sown them. Others take much longer.

7 A plant's first leaves come from inside the seed and are different to the leaves that grow afterward. Wait until your tiny seedlings have some true leaves and then thin them by carefully pulling some of them out, or snipping them off with a pair of scissors, to leave spaces between the ones that are left. The seed packet will tell you how much space. It may seem a waste, but plants that are too close together won't grow well because they are competing for light, water, and nutrients. It is easiest to pull them out when the soil is damp.

Planting Seeds Indoors 😊😊😊

Many seeds (beans, sweetcorn, squash) need to be warm to germinate (begin growing) and are best sown indoors in pots and then planted out in the garden later. Check the seed packet—it will tell you when you should begin sowing and how deep you should sow them.

You will need

Small pots

Seed tray

Potting mix (compost)

Watering can with fine rose

Seeds

Seed labels

Clear plastic bags

Elastic bands

Popsicle (lolly stick)

Trowel

1 Wash your pots and seed trays if they have been used before. Fill them almost to the top with potting mix (compost). Water with a fine rose to make sure the potting mix is damp.

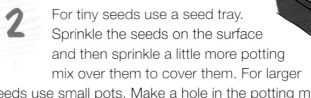

2 For tiny seeds use a seed tray. Sprinkle the seeds on the surface and then sprinkle a little more potting mix over them to cover them. For larger seeds use small pots. Make a hole in the potting mix with your finger (the seed packet will tell you how deep) and pop a seed into it. Then cover it over with potting mix.

3 Write the name of the seed you have planted on a seed label and push it into the potting mix—it's easy to forget which seeds are in which tray!

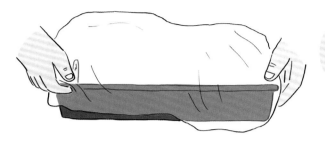

4 Water again with a little more water—don't get your seeds too wet or they will rot. Place the pots or seed tray in clear plastic bags and seal them with an elastic band. Put them on trays on a warm, sunny windowsill. As soon as the seedlings begin to show, you can remove the plastic bag. Keep the soil damp but not too wet.

5 If you have planted lots of small seeds in a seed tray, they need to be "pricked out" and "grown on" in small pots. The plants' first leaves come from inside the seed and are different to the leaves that grow afterward, which are called "true" leaves. Wait until your tiny seedlings have some true leaves before you repot then. Then fill some small pots with potting mix and make a hole with your finger in the center of each one.

6 Using a popsicle (lolly) stick or pencil, carefully loosen the soil around a seedling. Hold the seedling gently by its leaves (not the stem) and lift it onto the end of the popsicle stick, trying to keep some of the potting mix around the roots. Drop it into the hole in the pot and fill in the hole. Sometimes the stems are a bit weak so bury them a bit deeper—the potting mix will hold them upright.

7 Keep the pots on the windowsill until they are strong enough, and the weather is right, for them to be planted in your garden. It will be a shock for the little plants to go outside into the cold so "harden them off" by taking them out during the day and bringing them back at night. Do this for about a week before you plant them in the ground.

8 Before you plant them out, water them. Then dig a hole that is a little bigger than the plant pot. Hold one hand over the top of a pot with your finger and thumb around the plant's stem. Turn the pot over and the plant should slide out into your hands. You could pull it very gently if you need to. Some or all of the potting mix will still be clinging to the root. Lower the root ball into the hole. The top should be level with the soil in your plot. Fill in the spaces around the plant with soil and firm it down with your hands. Water it well.

Looking After Your Garden Plot

You may now have a garden full of healthy plants, but you still have a lot of gardening to do to keep them growing strong.

1 **Water** Water your plot every few days if the weather is dry. Watering well, with lots of water, every few days is better than a little every day.

2 **Keep out weeds** Weeds are your enemies because they take precious water and nutrients away from the plants you are growing. A hoe is your best weapon in the fight against them! Push your hoe forward, skimming the blade horizontally through the soil just below the surface, between rows of seeds or plants. Be careful not to damage the plants you are growing! Hoeing will cut the weeds in half. This will kill annual weeds (ones that grow from seed each year) and weaken perennial ones (ones that last from year to year). In small spaces, or to get rid of perennial weeds, dig out weed roots with a fork or trowel.

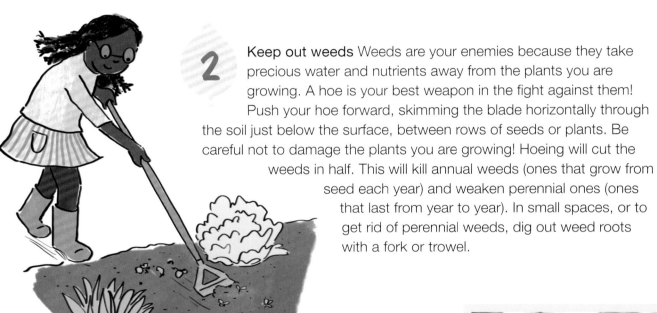

Hoeing tips

• It is best to hoe on warm, dry days—the weeds will dry out and won't grow again.

• Try to hoe your patch once a week to keep weeds down.

• Hoeing will break up the top surface of the soil so that when it rains, the rain soaks quickly into the soil and down to the plants' roots.

3 Feed your plants

Plants do not need to eat—they make all their food in their leaves in a process called photosynthesis. For this they need sun, water, carbon dioxide from the air, and green stuff in the leaves called chlorophyll. However, they do need nutrients to grow well in the same way that we need vitamins and minerals. They suck the nutrients up through their roots along with water. When you add manure or compost to the soil that will add lots of nutrients, but you can also use a tomato fertilizer. About once a week add some to the water in your watering can (look at the instructions on the bottle so you know how much to use)—but your plants won't die if you forget!

4 Support tall plants

Some plants that grow tall (e.g. sunflowers) need to be tied to canes to stop them from blowing over. Twisty plastic-covered wire plant ties are easiest for this as you can twist them together rather than tying knots, but you can use string or garden twine. Wind the string once or twice tightly around the cane and knot it in place. Then wrap it more loosely around the stem of the plant and knot it twice. It needs to be loose to allow the plant to grow. If you see that a tie has got too tight for a plant—cut it off!

5 **Control bugs** New young plants are very tasty food for many bugs. You must wage war on them! Slugs and snails are the biggest enemies of young plants and you can deal with them in lots of different ways.

• Walk around your plot, especially in the early morning, evening, or after rain and pick up slugs and snails. Drop them into a bucket of water, which will drown them—or take them away and release them in a wild place away from your plot or any other garden. Pick off other bugs like caterpillars at the same time—they often like to hide underneath leaves, so remember to check underneath, especially when you spot signs of nibbling.

• Cut some grapefruit in half and eat the fruit. Keep the skins and place them upside down around your plot. The slugs will crawl underneath and in the morning you can pick them up and put them in the bucket.

• Put a barrier around your plants. Try crushed shells (egg and sea shells). Slugs and snails don't like to crawl over them. A ring of copper tape or pipe will give slugs and snails a small electric shock and stop them crossing it. For young plants you can also cut the bottom off a plastic bottle and place it over the plant.

• Make a beer trap. Cut the top third off a plastic bottle. Turn it over and put it inside the bottom. Ask an adult for some beer to put in the bottom, then dig a hole for the bottle. Don't place it too deep otherwise creatures like beetles, which are your friends because they eat slugs, might fall in. Have the rim about 1 in (2.5 cm) above the level of the soil. Slugs love beer—they smell it, crawl in, and can't get out again.

• Encourage the good guys. Many bugs eat other bugs, such as ladybugs (ladybirds), which eat aphids. Insects such as bees are really important because they will pollinate your flowers. Help these bugs and others. Make a bug hotel and plant flowers that bees love to visit.

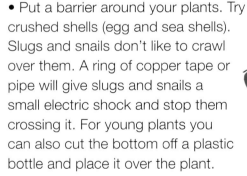

6 Scare off birds Many birds like to eat seeds and fruit; pigeons adore some green leaves. Fruit crops such as strawberries are best covered with a net, but you can also scare birds away with a bird scarer—they catch the light and scare the birds (see pages 87–89). You could even make a scarecrow with canes and old clothes (see pages 84–86).

7 Make compost Soil with compost in it has plenty of nutrients and it doesn't dry out as quickly so it is really good idea to make your own compost. You will need to get a compost bin and then ask everyone in the family to put in any waste that has come from a plant—lawn clippings, prunings, dead flower heads, carrot tops, vegetable peelings, fruit skins and cores (but not cooked food). Shredded paper and cardboard can also go in, as can pet bedding from rabbits or guinea pigs. After a few months everything will magically turn into compost, which you can spread on your plot.

Growing In Containers

Even if you don't have a garden you can still be a gardener and grow plants in containers, from cute little teacups for indoor plants to window boxes and larger pots for patios and porches—there are lots of lovely projects in Chapter 2. You can grow plants from seed (see pages 16–19), but if you want quicker results buy them from garden centers. Make sure you buy plants that look healthy and strong.

Planting up a container

1 Before you put your plants in your chosen container give them a good drink of water. Make sure that your container has some drainage holes. Put in a layer of stones or pieces of broken pot to stop the potting mix (compost) clogging up the holes.

2 Partly fill the container with potting mix. Sit one of the pots on the potting mix to see if the top of the pot reaches nearly to the top of the container. If it doesn't, add a bit more potting mix. Plan where you want to put your plants, try placing the pots in different positions around the container.

3 Now take the plants out of their pots. To do this, hold one hand over the top of a pot with your finger and thumb around the plant's stem. Turn the pot over and the plant should slide out into your hands. You could pull it very gently, but if it doesn't come free don't yank it! Instead slide a kitchen knife around the edge of the pot to loosen it.

4 Stand the root balls (which will be flowerpot-shaped) on the potting mix and fill in with more potting mix around them. The potting mix should be the same level as the top of the root ball and a little below the top of the container so that when you water your plants, the water won't run over the sides. Press the potting mix down around the plants with your fingers, making sure that the top of the potting mix is level.

5 If your container is going to be indoors you must stand it in a saucer or tray. When you water it, the water will drain through the holes and you don't want it spilling out onto the windowsill or table! Finally, water the container and place it somewhere where it gets plenty of light.

Looking after your plants

1 Remember to water your plants regularly—outdoor containers dry out quickly in warm weather. However, do not over-water. Most plants do not like growing in soggy potting mix (compost) so, for indoor plants, there should be no water standing in the tray underneath the pot.

2

About once a week add some liquid feed to the water in your jug to give your plants the nutrients they need (see page 21). The instructions on the bottle will tell you how much to use. More is not better—using too much can kill the plants!

3 If you are growing flowering plants, deadhead them. That means pull or snip off the flowers once they look as if they are dying. This will encourage the plant to grow new ones.

Plant Lists

There are thousands of different seed and plant varieties to choose from when you go along to your garden center, so which should you choose? Here is a list of some fun and exciting plants to try which are all easy to grow, whether you are planting them in a garden plot or a window box. Many of the projects in chapters that follow also have suggestions for which plants to use.

Salad bowl garden

- Lettuce 'Lollo Rosso'
- Spinach 'Bordeaux'—red stem, baby leaf
- Lettuce 'Mizuna'
- Scallion (spring onion)
- Cherry tomato 'Tumbler'
- Corn salad 'Pepite'
- Cucumber
- Lettuce 'Little Gem'
- Lamb's lettuce
- Edible carrot leaf—grown for leaves, not roots
- Mustard
- Radish
- Beets (beetroot) 'Bulls Blood'—grown for its leaves
- Tatsoi

Crazy fruit and vegetables

- Brussels sprouts 'Red Delicious'—purple sprouts
- Chard 'Bright Lights'—mix of white, red, pink, gold, and orange stems
- Strawberry 'Maxim'—fruit as big as a small hand
- Tomato 'Tigerella'—striped fruit
- Squash 'Turks Turban'
- Cranberry (borlotti) bean 'Lamon'—pink and white blotched pods and mottled beans
- French bean 'Purple King'—dwarf purple beans
- Cucumber 'Crystal Lemon'—round, yellow fruit
- Eggplant (aubergine) 'Mohican'—white fruit
- Carrot 'Purple Haze' (purple carrots)
- Sweetcorn 'Indian Summer'—white, red, purple, and yellow kernels on the same cob
- Sweetcorn 'Red Strawberry'—for popcorn
- Raspberry 'Allgold'—golden raspberries
- Beets (beetroot) 'Chioggia'—cut it open to reveal white and red rings
- Zucchini (courgette) 'One Ball'—round, orange fruit

Fast-growing seeds

- Radish
- Carrot 'Parmex'
- Arugula (rocket)
- Cress
- Spinach
- Turnip 'Arcoat'
- Beets (beetroot) 'Pronto'
- Nigella 'Miss Jekyll' (love-in-a-mist)
- Limnanthes (fried egg plant)
- Nasturtium
- California poppy
- Sunflowers

Scratch-and-sniff

- Lamb's ears
- Variegated sage 'Icterina'
- Woolly leaves
- Elephant's ears
- Feather grass
- Quaking grass
- Thyme
- Basil
- Cat's ear
- Daisy
- Bottlebrush
- Bronze fennel

chapter 2

Grow It Yourself

Tasty Herb Pot ☺ ☺ ○

There's nothing nicer than harvesting some of your own plants to cook with and growing herbs is a great way to begin. You can snip off a few leaves to add to an omelet, to flavor a roast chicken, or to sprinkle on a pizza! Herbs are very easy to grow in a window box on a sunny window ledge or patio. For a never-ending supply of tasty leaves, all you need to do is keep on picking them.

You will need

Large window box

Stones or large pieces of broken terracotta pot

Potting mix (compost) suitable for growing herbs—this will usually have some sand or grit mixed into it

Small trowel

Selection of herbs to fill your trough—you could use any of these: parsley, chives, rosemary, oregano, thyme, basil, sage (miniature varieties do best in window boxes)

Watering can

1 Before filling your window box with potting mix, cover the drainage holes in the base. Use large stones or pieces of broken terracotta pot. This will allow water to drain away, but prevent the holes from getting clogged up with potting mix (compost). It will also prevent the potting mix spilling out through the holes and onto surfaces.

2 Cover the base of your container with about ½ in (1 cm) of potting mix, breaking any large clods apart with your hands. Smooth off the surface with your fingers.

Hints and tips

• Keep picking your herbs and the plants will keep growing new leaves.

• Always keep the container well watered—don't let it dry out and add some fertilizer every few weeks.

• Mint is a great herb to grow but it gets big quite quickly and might squeeze out the other plants, so it would be better in its own pot.

3 Take your plants out of their containers (see page 19) and arrange them in the window box. Upright plants will look better in the center of the container, while creeping plants are best tumbling over the ends.

4 Once you are happy with your display, fill the gaps around the plants with potting mix, leaving a level surface about 1 in (2.5 cm) below the top of the trough. Firm around the plants with your fingertips and water them well.

5 Ask an adult to help you lift the box onto a sunny windowsill. It will be heavy!

Just keep on **PICKING!**

Strawberry Planter

Picking plump and juicy strawberries is a summer treat. They are much tastier than shop-bought ones and it's easy to grow your own in a special strawberry planter, which has holes or "pockets" around the sides. For lots of berries, put the planter in a sunny spot and keep it well watered. Plant strawberries in spring for a juicy summer crop.

You will need

Large strawberry planter (with a drainage hole in the bottom)

Stones or pieces of broken terracotta pot

Multi-purpose potting mix (compost)

Strawberry plants (enough to fill all the pockets and one for the top)

Trowel

Watering can

Liquid tomato fertilizer (optional)

1

Cover the drainage hole at the bottom of the pot with a stone to stop it from clogging. Add potting mix (compost) to just below the level of the first pocket and pat down with your fingers.

 2 Remove one of the strawberry plants from its pot by holding it firmly around the stem and gently pulling it out of its container.

Who can RESIST those juicy berries?

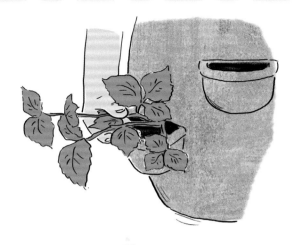

3 Put the strawberry plant into one of the pockets. Push the potting mix around the roots but don't cover the crown of the plant (where the shoots come from the soil).

4 Add more soil and plant the other pockets. Finish off by putting a strawberry plant in the top and fill the gaps around it with potting mix. Leave a 1-in (2.5-cm) gap between the top of the potting mix and the lip of the pot.

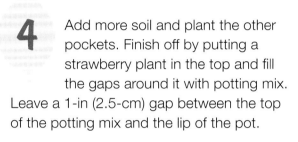

5 Water the planter well, so the roots are soaked. Water the top of the planter, not each pocket, as you could wash the soil out and leave the roots exposed.

Hints and tips

• Strawberries are thirsty plants so they will need regular watering, especially during hot and dry weather.

• Turn the pot around occasionally, so that each side gets some sunshine (this way your plants will grow evenly).

• You'll get better, bigger strawberries if you feed the plants once a week after they come into flower. Add a few drops of liquid tomato fertilizer to your watering can when you water the plants.

Eggshell Gardens

The next time your family has boiled eggs for breakfast, ask everyone to eat their egg very carefully so that they do not break the shells—then you can fill them with miniature flowers and moss to make a tiny garden.

You will need

Eggs

Knife

Bowl

Potting mix (compost)

Garden sieve (optional)

Egg cups or egg carton

Pin

Spoon

Moss (available from florists)

Plants with small roots:

Forget-me-nots

Krauss' spikemoss

Violets 'Moonlight'

Sweet violets

1 You can either eat boiled eggs and keep the shells or ask an adult to help you cut the tops off raw eggs using a knife. Do this over a bowl so you can tip the raw egg out—you can use it to make an omelet later!

2 Rinse the empty eggshells carefully in warm water.

3 Check that your potting mix (compost) isn't lumpy. If it is, you can push a little of the mix through a garden sieve, if you have one, or use your fingers to break up any lumps.

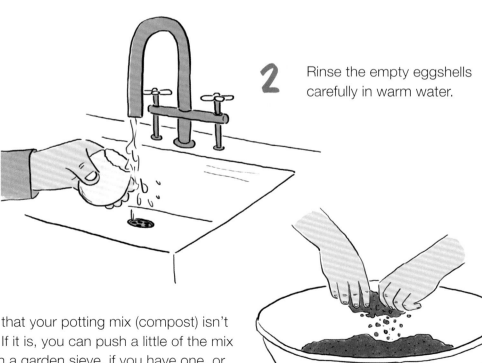

4 Place the each eggshell upside down in an egg cup or carton and very carefully make a few small holes in the bottom of each egg with the pin. This is so that the water can drain away.

5 Put the eggshells the right way round in the egg cups or carton. Spoon a little potting mix (compost) into each egg, making sure that there will be enough room for the plants.

6 Put one plant in each egg and add a little more potting mix. Gently push a small piece of moss onto the top of the potting mix if you wish.

Hints and tips

• The potting mix will dry out quickly, so water the eggshells every day with just a little water.

• Flowers like violets will carry on flowering for a few weeks so "deadhead" them by pinching off any faded flowers. This will encourage new ones to grow.

EggCITING project!

Dainty Teacups

You can often buy old teacups and saucers very cheaply in charity shops or garage sales. Collect a few of these and create a pretty garden to brighten up your desk, windowsill, or shelf. Adding gravel to the potting mix will stop the plants becoming waterlogged and keep them healthy.

You will need

Plastic bowl

Potting mix (compost)

Fine gravel

An old tablespoon

Teacups and saucers

Tiny plants with small roots:

Thrift

Clematis marmoraria

Winter aconite

Fritillary

Primrose

Saxifrage

Stonecrop

Hints and tips

• Choose alpines or small-scale plants for your teacups.

• Plant tiny bulbs, such as snowdrops, dwarf narcissi, or grape hyacinths in the winter so that you will have a pretty floral display in spring.

1 In the bowl combine potting mix (compost) with the same amount of fine gravel. Use the spoon and for each spoonful of potting mix, add one spoonful of gravel. How much you need depends on the number of cups and plants you have but don't use all the gravel—you'll need some for the next stage and at the end.

2 Put about a tablespoon of fine gravel in the bottom of each of the teacups.

Tiny TEACUP gardens

3 Spoon some of the potting mix and gravel mixture into the first cup, to come about one-third of the way up the cup (you need to leave enough room for the plant!).

4 Take the plant out of its plastic pot (see page 19) and gently shake off any excess potting mix. Hold the plant in the middle of the cup and fill round the edges with more potting mix. Press the potting mix down gently with your fingers so that the plant sits firmly in place. Plant the remaining teacups in the same way.

 5 Sprinkle some more fine gravel over the surface of the potting mix in each cup, making sure that it is completely covered.

6 Water each cup carefully with just a little water, making sure that the potting mix is damp but not completely drenched. Alpine plants do not like to sit in water! Check the potting mix every couple of days and if it feels dry water it, but only a little at a time. Pick off any dead flower heads as they appear (this is known as "deadheading") to encourage the plant to make new flowers.

Shopping Baskets

Even if you only have a small garden—or even no garden at all—you can still create a beautiful border in some colorful shopping baskets. These are made from bright woven plastic that will withstand rain or shine and create a blaze of color wherever they are positioned.

You will need

Black plastic refuse sacks for lining the baskets

Scissors

Woven plastic baskets

Stones or large pieces of broken terracotta pot

Trowel

Potting mix (compost)

Moisture-retaining granules (optional)

Plants with small roots:

Lady's mantle

Caraway

Tickseed 'Early Sunrise'

Cosmos 'Sonata Carmine' and 'Sonata White'

Avens

English lavender

Orchid primrose

Balkan clary

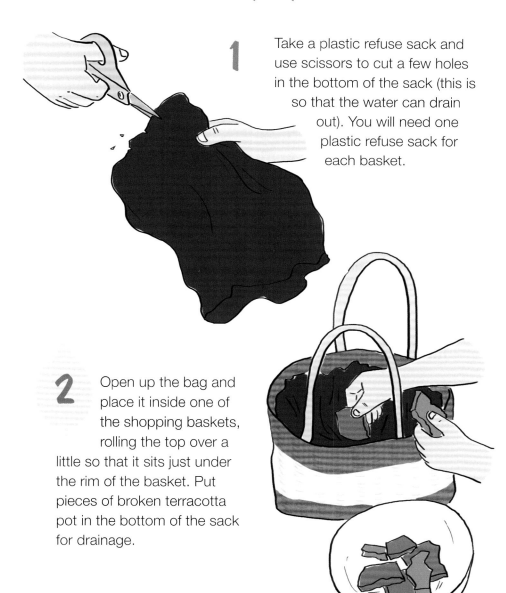

1 Take a plastic refuse sack and use scissors to cut a few holes in the bottom of the sack (this is so that the water can drain out). You will need one plastic refuse sack for each basket.

2 Open up the bag and place it inside one of the shopping baskets, rolling the top over a little so that it sits just under the rim of the basket. Put pieces of broken terracotta pot in the bottom of the sack for drainage.

3 Use a trowel to shovel potting mix (compost) into the bag until it is about half full. Add a few handfuls of moisture-retaining granules, if you wish.

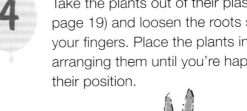

4 Take the plants out of their plastic pots (see page 19) and loosen the roots slightly with your fingers. Place the plants in the basket, arranging them until you're happy with their position.

5 Add more potting mix around the plants and firm it down with your fingers. Give the basket a good soak with water.

Hints and tips

• Water the baskets regularly, giving a good soaking every few days in warm weather rather than a little water daily.

• Deadhead regularly to encourage more flowers and use a general-purpose fertilizer (see page 21) every couple of weeks.

Baskets of COLOR!

Potato Planter

Potatoes are the most exciting vegetables to grow as you just don't know what is going on under the soil. Pull them up and you find a treasure trove of tubers (potatoes) to mash, roast, boil, or bake. They are really easy to grow in a large container so plant some seed potatoes in spring, and you'll be eating a tasty crop in the summer.

You will need

Large, deep planter, at least 12 in (30 cm) wide (we used a metal wastebasket)

Drill and drill bit

Seed potatoes

Cardboard egg carton

Multi-purpose potting mix (compost)

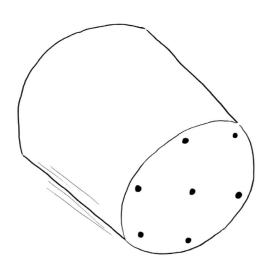

1 First prepare your planter. Most garden pots have holes in their base to allow water to drain away. This stops the growing potatoes from rotting. If you are using a wastebasket, ask an adult to help you drill some holes in the base.

2 When you buy your seed potatoes in late winter, you need to sprout them before planting. Place a single potato into the hollow of a cardboard egg carton, making sure that the end with the most eyes (little indents where buds will grow) faces upward. Put in a light, cool place until the sprouts are about 1 in (2.5 cm) high. This sprouting stage may take up to six weeks.

Hints and tips

• Potatoes grow best in a warm and sunny spot.

• Keep plants well watered—never let the soil dry out.

• It's essential to keep on adding soil to cover the growing shoots, or your potatoes will be green and inedible.

• There are lots of potato varieties available, some of which produce larger tubers that need to stay in the soil until late summer.

3 When your potatoes have sprouted, and any chance of frost has passed, it's time to plant them! Add a layer of potting mix (compost) about 4 in (10 cm) deep to your planter. Stand the sprouted tubers on top, with the sprouts pointing upward and spaced apart, and cover them with another 4 in (10 cm) of potting mix. Water well.

4 When the potato shoots are about 6 in (15 cm) tall (which will take several weeks), cover the stems with potting mix, allowing the tips to just poke above the surface. As the stems grow, keep adding more potting mix until you are left with a 4-in (10-cm) gap between the surface of the potting mix and the top of the pot.

5 Your potatoes will be ready for picking in midsummer, after the plants have flowered. Loosen the potting mix with your hands and pull the plants up. There should be plenty of potatoes attached to the roots and more hidden in the soil.

Pots and pots of POTS!

Budding Bunny Ears ◕○○

The cut-off ends of carrots can carry on growing fresh leaves. Just keep them well watered in a sunny spot and you'll have sprouting bunny ears in a week or two. You could even plant your sprouted carrot tops in the garden. They will eventually form little flowers and later seeds, which you can collect and sow to grow, you guessed it, more carrots!

You will need

Scissors

Small plastic water bottle

Sandpaper

Paintbrush

Water-based acrylic or eggshell paint (in any color you like)

Pieces of black and white felt

White (PVA) glue

Pompom

Googly eyes

String

A little sand

A large spoon

1 large carrot

Sharp knife and chopping board

Small pitcher (jug)

1 Use pointy scissors to cut the top off a small plastic water bottle—you may need to ask an adult to help you. Make sure that you keep both parts as well as the screw-top lid. Rub the sandpaper all over the bottle to roughen up the plastic. This will help the paint stick to the plastic surface.

2 Decide what color paint to use for your bunny and paint the outside of both the top and bottom of the bottle. If the paint looks streaky, paint on another coat but remember to let the paint dry between each coat.

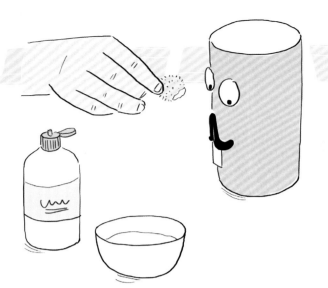

3 When the paint has dried, cut out the shapes for the bunny's eyes, mouth, and teeth from the pieces of felt. Glue these to the bottom part of the bottle and then glue on the pompom nose in between. Don't forget to glue on the googly eyes as well. (Keep the top part of the bottle—and the lid—for later.)

4 Cut some short pieces of string for the whiskers. Pour a little glue into a saucer, roll the pieces of string in the glue, and then stick the whiskers on either side of your bunny's mouth.

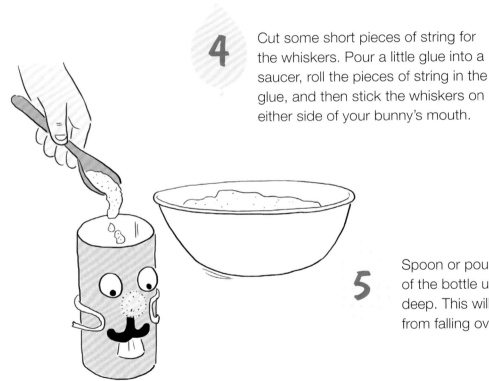

5 Spoon or pour some sand into the bottom of the bottle until it is about 2 in (5 cm) deep. This will make it heavier and stop it from falling over too easily.

6 Screw the lid on to the top part of the bottle. Holding it upside down, spoon in the sand until it is almost full—this is for the carrot top to grow in. Put the top of the bottle inside the bottom of the bottle.

7 Carefully cut the top off the carrot, making sure that the carrot top is about 1 in (2.5 cm) long.

8 Put the carrot top on the sand and then fill up this part of the bottle with water using the small pitcher (jug). Place the finished bunny on a light windowsill. Keep the water topped up and you will see new "ears" begin to shoot within a day or two.

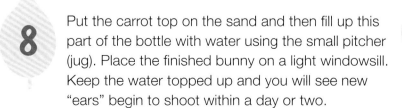

Seaside Garden

Next time you are at the seaside make a collection of shells and pretty pebbles to make this seaside garden—or you may already have some from your last visit. You need quite a lot of tiny ones and some larger ones. A blue-and-white enamel bowl makes the perfect container to plant your seaside garden in, but any large flat bowl will do—even an old washing up bowl. You don't have to choose plants that grow by the sea—unless you live by the sea, of course! Instead, use plants with whitish leaves, which will conjure up the "feel" of the seaside.

You will need

Large enamel dish or other large flat bowl

Drill and drill bit

Stones or large pieces of broken terracotta pot

Potting mix (compost)

Gravel

3–4 plants depending on the size of your bowl—they need to be spaced out so you can see the pebbles and shells

Miniature shells

Pebbles

Large shells

Plants with small roots:

African lily 'Charlotte'

Sea thrift 'Splendens'

Cornflower 'Silver Feather'

Beach aster 'Sea Breeze'

Garden lotus 'Fire Vine'

1 If your bowl doesn't have holes in the bottom you will need to make some so that water can drain away. Ask an adult to drill a few holes in the bottom of the bowl.

2 Cover the holes with a few pieces of terracotta pot for drainage.

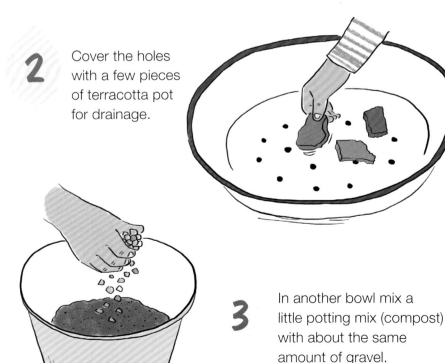

3 In another bowl mix a little potting mix (compost) with about the same amount of gravel.

4

Put a few handfuls of gravel in the bottom of the dish and then add a layer of the gravel and potting mix mixture you have just made. (This will help to improve drainage.) Half-fill the dish with more plain potting mix.

Oh I do like to be beside the SEASIDE!

5   Take the plants out of their plastic pots (see page 19) and arrange them in the dish, spacing them out as equally as you can. Hold each plant upright as you add more potting mix around it. Fill the dish so it is level, firming it around the plants with your fingers.

Tip

Sprinkle some small pebbles over the potting mix if you haven't got any miniature shells. You can buy these from garden centers and garden supply stores.

6

Sprinkle the miniature shells all over the surface of the potting mix to cover it and arrange the pebbles and large shells around the plants. Water the plants. In hot weather you may have to water the bowl every day but don't let it get waterlogged.

Fairy Rings

Add some magic to your lawn in the spring by planting crocus bulbs to create your very own fairy rings. You may have to sneak a peak in the dark to see the fairies, but the rings are still a great place for having a picnic and playing. Best of all, the flowers will appear again every spring.

You will need

Piece of string, about 25 in (65 cm) in length

Tent peg

Plastic water bottle

Play sand

Special bulb planter

About 30 crocus bulbs

1 In late fall (autumn), choose an flat, open area of lawn for your fairy circle—ask first—some people are very proud of their lawns! Tie one end of the piece of string to the tent peg and push this into the middle of your chosen area of lawn. Fill the plastic bottle with some play sand and tie the other end of the string to its neck. Carefully tip out a line of sand as you move the string around in a circle, keeping it tight all the time. This will mark out your fairy ring.

2 Use the bulb planter to make a hole on the chalk line. Push and twist the bulb planter into the soil until it has gone in about 2 in (5 cm) below the surface of the grass. Then twist it again and pull it out—you may need to ask an adult to help you if the ground is very hard. A plug of soil will stay in the planter. Many planters have a squeeze handle—squeeze it and it will release the soil plug. (If yours doesn't do this, the plug will come out when you make the next hole.) Leave the "plug" of soil and grass by the side of the hole. Now make another hole about 4 in (10 cm) from the first and continue around the circle like this.

Garden MAGIC

3 Place a crocus bulb in each hole, making sure that the bulb is the right way up (the pointed end should be facing upward). Replace the plug of soil and grass, and firm it down well. The bulbs will grow through the grass the following spring.

Tip

Make sure that the crocus ring section of the lawn is not cut until about six weeks after the plants have finished flowering. This gives the plant a chance to put the energy from its old leaves back into the bulb, ready to grow again next year.

Edible Garden

This cute little garden is beautiful and tasty! Buy small "plug" plants (which have already been grown from seed) from the garden center to plant up your container. Choose small varieties which will not grow too big for your trug.

You will need

Metal trug

Stones or large pieces of broken terracotta pot

Gravel

Potting mix (compost)

Moisture-retaining granules (optional)

Watering can

Liquid tomato fertilizer (optional)

Plants with small roots:

Pot marigold

Strawberry 'Sarian F1' and 'Merlan F1'

Sunflower 'Teddy Bear'

Red-leaved lettuce

Cherry tomato 'Microtom', 'Tiny Tim', or 'Red Robin'

Purple basil

Parsley

Radish 'Cherry Belle'

1 If there are no drainage holes in the base of the trug ask an adult to drill some. Cover the holes with a few stones or pieces of terracotta pot and then cover with a layer of gravel.

2 Put some potting mix (compost) into the trug, adding a few of handfuls of moisture-retaining granules if you have some, which will help prevent the trug drying out.

Tip

You can eat sunflower seeds! When the flowers are dying, they will start to flop over from the weight of the seeds. Cut off the seed head and bring it indoors to dry. After about 3–4 days, shake the seeds out. Wash and dry before eating.

3 Carefully remove the sunflower from its plastic pot (see page 19). Hollow out a space in the potting mix toward the back of the trug and position the sunflower plant in it.

A trug full of TASTINESS

4 Arrange all the other plants around the sunflower, cramming in as many as you can and pressing the potting mix in firmly around the plants. Carry your trug to a sunny sheltered place and give all the plants a good watering. Feed the plants, especially the strawberry and tomato plants, with a liquid tomato fertilizer to produce lots of fruits.

Salad Patch

A good way to start gardening is with a patch of garden where you can create a bed of favorite salad vegetables and flowers—although some plants such as tomatoes need warm weather so check if they grow well in your area. Include a bamboo teepee to provide support for climbing beans or peas. You don't need much space—a yard-square (meter-square) plot will do. It's a good idea to create a planting pattern on paper before you plant in the soil. You don't need to do it all on one day—gardening can be hard work!

You will need

Well-rotted manure

Spade/fork

Gloves

Rain (wellington) boots

Rake

5 garden stakes

Garden twine

Trowel

Watering can

Plants:

5 x pole beans (climbing French beans or runner beans)

4 x tomato plants (tumbling variety)

4 x corn

1 x chard

1 x zucchini (courgette)

1 x nasturtium

1 x lettuce

16 x French marigolds

1 In the spring, ask an adult where you can start your garden and mark out your space with some canes or sticks. First dig over the soil and pull out all the weeds. To give your plants a boost, spread manure all over the soil evenly and lightly dig it in with a spade or fork. It's important to remember to always wear gloves when you handle manure. Now roughly level the surface with a rake (see pages 13–15).

2 Wearing a pair of boots or sturdy shoes, walk up and down all over the entire bed, putting all your weight on your heels so you push down and compact the soil. This means there will be no uneven lumps or bumps in the bed.

Hints and tips

• Slugs and snails will greedily munch through salad crops. Hunt them down by regularly checking the undersides of leaves and removing them (see page 22).

• You don't have to follow our plan exactly. Colorful lettuces, arugula (rocket), scallions (spring onions), beets (beetroot), radishes, and carrots are easy to grow, and peas can be trained up shorter teepees.

• Apart from adding lots of color to a bed, many flowers, such as nasturtium, calendula (pot marigold), and viola are edible and can be added to salads, while French marigolds are useful to attract pesky whiteflies away from more precious (and tasty!) plants.

Grow your OWN veg!

3 Rake the trodden-down soil back and forth, so there are no big clods or lumps of soil and the surface is nice and smooth. Remove any big stones that have worked their way to the surface.

4 Make a bamboo teepee at the center of the bed. Evenly space five stakes in a circle and push them firmly into the soil, to a depth of about 4 in (10 cm). You might have to ask a grown-up to help, as it can be hard to push in the stakes.

5 Gather the tops of the stakes together in your hand, cut a long length of garden twine, and then bind the stakes together to finish your teepee. Unless you are very tall, you'll probably need to ask a grown-up to help with this, as well!

6 Start by planting your beans. Dig a hole with a trowel and carefully plant one bean seedling at the base of each stake. Wind the long shoot all the way around the stake, to help it start to climb (if necessary, you can keep it in place with a loosely tied piece of twine).

7 Newly planted seedlings can wilt very quickly, so remember always to water them straight after planting. Use a watering can with a narrow spout and water the plants directly above the root area, so they get a really good soaking.

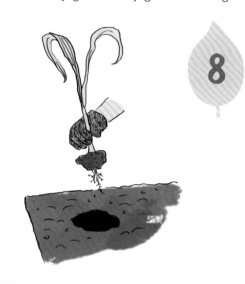

8 Once you've planted the beans, plant your tomatoes, putting one in the middle of each side of the bed. Dig a hole about 4 in (10 cm) from the edge of the bed, and plant a tomato plant (if you live in a cool area you may want to plant more of the other plants instead). Repeat for the three remaining sides.

9 Now you can plant your corn. Dig a hole at each corner of the bed and plant the corn, making sure the roots are well covered with soil. Water well and repeat for each corner.

10 Use the chard, nasturtium, and lettuce plants to fill the gaps left between the corn and the teepee. Now plant the marigolds at even intervals around the edges of the bed. Finish by giving everything a good watering.

11 Don't forget to water your plants in dry weather and pull out or hoe away any weeds.

Wildflower Bucket ⊙⊙⊙

These days everyone is trying to do their bit for nature—especially for bees. They help us by pollinating the flowers which grow into fruit and vegetables and we need to help them by giving them the wildflowers and nectar they love. Not many of us have room for a whole wildflower meadow, but how about having your own mini wildflower patch to carry around?

You will need

Plastic or metal bucket

Drill and drill bit (optional)

Gravel or large stones

Potting mix (compost)

Selection of annual wildflower seeds, such as corncockle, corn chamomile, and field cornflower—or you can buy packets of mixed wildflower seeds

Small plate

Watering can with a fine rose

Tip

After the wildflowers have finished flowering, you can leave them to form seedheads. Then collect the seeds and keep them somewhere dry, dark, and cool ready for sowing the following year.

1 Ask an adult to puncture or drill several holes in the bottom of your bucket. Add some gravel or large stones to the bottom of the bucket to help with drainage.

2 Fill the bucket with lots of potting mix (compost), firming it down with your hands as you go. You may need to ask your adult to help you tip the heavy bag of potting mix into the bucket.

3 Put a selection of wildflower seeds on the small plate and mix them up with your fingers. Sow the seeds by sprinkling them over the surface of the potting mix.

4 Gently sprinkle a little more of the potting mix over the top of the newly sown seeds, so they are just covered and no more.

Go wild for WILDFLOWERS!

5 Water the seeds well before placing the bucket somewhere sunny. Remember to put a fine rose over the spout of your watering can so that you don't disturb the potting mix around the new seeds.

6 As the seeds grow, you'll need to thin them out to give the new seedlings plenty of room in which to grow strong. They grow best when there is about 4 in (10 cm) between each plant. Gently hold the seedling you want to keep without crushing it and lightly jiggle the seedling next to it until it comes away from the soil.

Terrific Terrariums

This lovely project shows that you don't even need a garden to grow lots of plants—just a large glass container. A terrarium is like an aquarium, but with soil instead of water, and plants instead of fish! These mini gardens look great when placed on a windowsill or shelf.

You will need

Large glass container such as a Kilner jar (a wide top is easier than a narrow one)

Expanded clay pellets (you can find these in garden centers)

Horticultural charcoal

Multi-purpose potting mix (compost)

Long-handled spoon

Watering can

Enough plants to fill your container—use tiny specimens of creeping fig, parlor palm, prayer plant, creeping Jenny, polka dot plant, or mind-your-own-business. Avoid cacti or plants grown for their flowers.

1 If the jar is dirty, wash it carefully in warm soapy water, then rinse it and dry it—you want to be able to see the plants! Now slowly pour in the expanded clay pellets to make a 2-in (5-cm) drainage layer in the base of the jar.

2 If potting mix (compost) is always wet it can become smelly, so add a thin layer of horticultural charcoal over the clay pellets, which will keep it fresh.

3 Fill a quarter of the container with potting mix and firmly press it down with your knuckles (if your wrist can't fit easily through the neck of the bottle, use the back of a long-handled spoon to press the potting mix down).

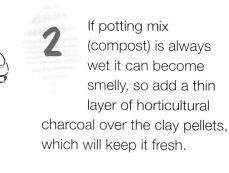

4 Use the long-handled spoon to dig small planting holes in the potting mix.

5 Carefully, lower your chosen plants into the holes you have dug. Firm the potting mix around the roots with the spoon. When you have finished planting, drop in some more clay pellets to fill any bare patches.

6 Pour water gently into the jar until the potting mix is thoroughly wet. If you leave the jar open you will need to water the potting mix regularly, but if you close the lid water cannot escape and the plants will keep recycling it.

Tip

If you are growing plants in a jar with the lid closed, the glass may sometimes get misted with condensation. If it does, open the lid for a few minutes until it clears.

A garden in a **JAR!**

Tyrannosaurus Garden

Ferns have been growing for millions of years. In fact, they are as old as the dinosaurs themselves! Use them alongside "rock" mountains and "moss" floors to create your very own prehistoric landscape in a cleverly decorated old tire, then hide your toy dinosaurs amongst them.

You will need

Old car tire

Warm, soapy water

Orange acrylic paint

Paint dish

Small paint roller or piece of sponge

Black plastic sack

Scissors

Garden fork

Potting mix (compost)

2–3 fern plants or other small leafy plants, such as holly ferns, Polypody fern, and Heuchera 'Beauty Color'

Watering can

2–3 large rocks or pebbles

Moss (real or sisal)

Selection of small plastic dinosaurs

Small paintbrush

1 Give the tire a good wash with some warm, soapy water and allow it dry. Put some orange acrylic paint in the paint dish and use the paint roller or small piece of sponge to apply it around the outside of the tire. You will need to add a few coats to build up the color, allowing the paint to dry in between each coat.

2 Find a nice shady spot for your old tire (ferns don't like to be planted in the sun). Take the black plastic sack and cut a circle that is bigger than the whole tire so that it is big enough to cover the base of the tire and go up inside and over the rim. Tuck inside the inner ring.

Create your own JURASSIC park!

3 Use a garden fork to puncture some holes in the plastic. You may want to ask an adult to help you with this. Putting holes in the plastic will allow water to drain slowly from the tire, keeping the soil quite moist but not soaking wet.

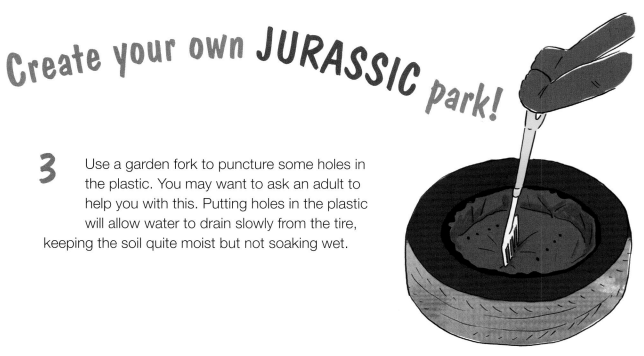

4 Fill the tire with some potting mix (compost), making sure that you push it right into the inside ring of the tire as well as the center. If you push some into the inside ring first, this will help to hold the plastic in place. When your tire is half-full, take the plants carefully out of their pots (see page 19) and arrange them inside the tire until you are happy with the layout.

5 Fill the remaining space in the tire with some more of the potting mix, firming it down as you go along, and then water the plants in well.

6 Arrange the rocks or pebbles in your prehistoric world, cover any areas of potting mix that are showing with some moss, and then introduce your dinosaurs to their new home. Use the small paintbrush to add some rivers of orange volcanic larva to one of the stones.

Tip

If you do not have enough space in your garden, you can put your tire on a hard area such as paving or gravel. If you do this, lay the section of plastic sack over a piece of grass or earth when you are puncturing it with the fork before putting it in the tire.

Sunflower Alley

Gigantic sunflowers are great to look at, but even better to walk through! Plant them on either side of a pathway and you can make a towering flower alley. The bees will love them and they will impress your friends and family.

You will need

20 small plastic pots

Potting mix (compost)

Sunflower seeds

Watering can with a fine rose

Bricks or small stone slabs

Trowel

About 20 strong bamboo canes

Garden twine or string

1 In spring, plant your sunflower seeds in small pots so that they can begin growing on a warm, sunny windowsill. Fill each small pot with potting mix (compost) and firm this down. Make a small hole with your finger, about ¾ in (2 cm) deep, drop in a sunflower seed, and then cover it over and firm down the potting mix before watering in well.

2 Leave the pots on a sunny windowsill and wait for them to grow! Water them regularly —but not too much—to prevent the potting mix drying out. After about 7–10 days you will start to see some shoots appearing.

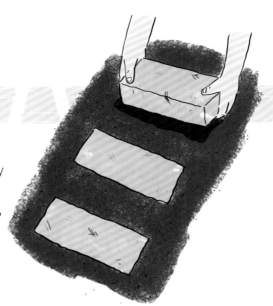

3 Start to prepare your planting area. On a patch of sunny ground, about 10 x 3 ft (3 x 1 m), place the bricks or small slabs to form a pathway. When they are in position, dig holes and drop them in so that they are level with the soil. Fill in and firm down the soil around them.

4 Once the sunflowers are about 8 in (20 cm) tall and all danger of frost has passed, harden them off (see page 19) and plant them out. Make sure that the two lines of sunflowers are at least 3 ft (1 m) apart. This will give you enough room to run through them when they have grown.

5 For each plant, dig a hole with the trowel about twice the size of its pot. Carefully remove the plant (see page 19) and put it in the hole, backfilling and firming the soil around it. Plant the next sunflower about 12 in (30 cm) further along and keep doing this until all are planted. Water them well.

6 When your sunflowers reach about 3 ft (1 m) in height, insert a bamboo cane next to each one and use the garden twine or string to tie the stem carefully to the cane in a figure-of-eight pattern. This will help to keep your sunflowers upright in strong winds. Loosen the ties as the stems get thicker so that they don't cut into them.

7 It is important to keep your sunflowers well watered, especially during hot, sunny spells. If you are going to be away, then ask a kind neighbor to water your sunflowers for you. When you come home, they will have grown even taller!

Tips

• Slugs and snails love to eat young sunflower plants—you will need to protect them when you first plant them out (see page 22).

• Sometimes young sunflower plants are a bit floppy so you may need to tie them to a small stick when you first plant them outside.

• After the flowers have died let the seeds ripen, then cut off the heads and hang them in a dry, airy place, such as a garage, to dry out. Then hang them on your bird feeder. The birds will love to feast on them through the winter.

Watch tiny seeds turn into GIANT sunflowers

Halloween Pumpkins ☺☺☺

When Halloween comes around what could be more fun than carving a pumpkin that you have grown yourself and have just picked from your garden. Pumpkins are great to grow as you can watch them get bigger and bigger and bigger. Then, not only can you carve them, but you can also make delicious pumpkin pie or pumpkin soup and roast the seeds for a tasty snack—nothing is wasted! Some pumpkins grow until they are truly enormous, but you need a very big garden for this kind and they don't make good lanterns.

You will need

3 flowerpots, each 3 in (8 cm) in diameter

Potting mix (compost)

Pumpkin seeds (Jack O'Lantern or Jack-of-all-trades are good Halloween varieties)

3 transparent plastic bags (food or freezer bags work well)

3 elastic bands

A well-dug plot of garden 1–2 yards (meters) square

Spade

Well-rotted compost or manure

Trowel

Large plastic bottle

Scissors

Watering can

Wooden board

Sharp knife

1 In late spring, sow your pumpkin seeds (see page 18). Fill each flowerpot with potting mix (compost) and make a hole in each pot of potting mix with your finger about 1 in (2.5 cm) deep. Pop a seed into the hole, placing it on its side. (You will only need one plant but it's best to have some spares in case one doesn't grow.) Water the pots but don't get the potting mix too soggy.

2 Put each pot inside a transparent plastic bag and seal it with an elastic band. Place the pots on a sunny, warm windowsill—the temperature needs to be 68–77°F (20–25°C)—until the seeds germinate (begin to grow). This will take 5–7 days.

3 Once the seeds have germinated, take the pots out of the bags. Keep checking that the potting mix is damp and water them when they need it. Keep the plants inside for about 4 weeks or until the weather has warmed up and there is no more risk of frost, then gradually harden them off (see page 19) for 7–10 days by taking them outside during the day and back inside at night.

4 Pumpkins like to be planted in spots that are sunny for at least six hours a day and are sheltered from the wind, so choose your planting place carefully. Prepare the soil by using a spade to dig a hole about 16 in (40 cm) across and 16 in (40 cm) deep where you are going to plant your pumpkin (you may need to ask an adult to help you with this bit!). Fill it with potting mix or manure. Pile soil over the top to make a little mound about 6 in (15 cm) high for your plant.

5 Choose the strongest and healthiest of your three plants and water it. Use a trowel to dig a hole, which is a little bigger than the plant pot (see page 19) in the top of the mound. Hold your hand over the top of the pot, with your finger and thumb around the stalk, and turn the pot over. The plant should slide out into your hand.

6 Place the root ball into the hole and then fill it in with soil. The soil should be the same level as the top of the root ball. Firm the soil down with your hands and water it well. Keep your other two plants for a few days until you are sure that your pumpkin is growing strongly outside and you know you won't need them. Then give them away to some friends!

7 Use scissors to cut the bottom off a large plastic bottle (ask an adult to help you if you find this difficult) and place it over the top of your pumpkin plant. The bottle will protect the plant from slugs, snails, and cold weather until it is bigger and stronger but it will soon grow too big for the bottle! Lift the bottle off to water it and take the top off in the daytime so it doesn't get too hot. Keep it well watered while it is still small. Pumpkins have deep roots and can usually find their own water as they get bigger, but it is good to water them in very dry weather.

8 As it grows the pumpkin will produce long stems or vines, which you can gently wind in circles around the plant so they don't spread too far.

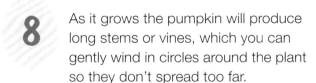

9 After a while the pumpkin will begin to flower. It will produce male and female flowers. Female flowers have a bump at the bottom, which will grow into a pumpkin, but often the first few flowers are all male and just have a straight stem. Pumpkin flowers are normally pollinated by bees or other insects flying from flower to flower, carrying pollen on their legs. However, if, after it has been flowering for a while, you can't see any pumpkins beginning to grow you may need to hand-pollinate them. To do this, pick a single male flower and remove its petals. Press it against the center of each female flower.

10 You will want to grow the largest pumpkin possible for your Halloween lantern. To make sure that some do grow really big, choose just two or three pumpkins to keep on growing and cut off any other baby ones. This will mean that all the plant's energy will go into your special pumpkins.

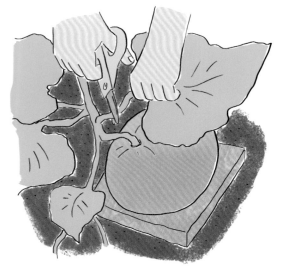

11 Big pumpkins that sit on wet soil sometimes begin to rot. Raise them up off the soil with a piece of board or a pile of straw. You can also help them ripen by cutting off any leaves that are shading them.

Happy HALLOWEEN!

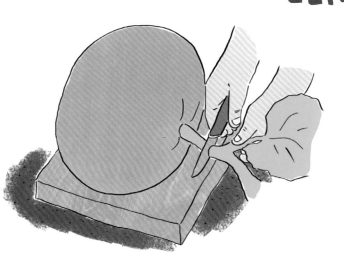

12 Leave your pumpkins on the plant for as long as possible until the skin has hardened and the fruits have started to crack near to the stem, but be sure to harvest them before the first frost. Ask an adult to help you cut each fruit from the stem with a sharp knife, leaving several inches of the stem attached.

chapter 3
Garden Decorations

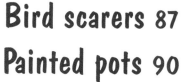

Plastic Bag Bunting

When winter comes and the flowers have all died, you could brighten up your garden with this fun bunting—or you could use it for a party in the summer. It is quick and easy to make and best of all reuses plastic bags which cause problems for the environment. Use any old plastic bags in bright colors to make bunting, which will withstand all weathers.

You will need

Thin cardstock—an old cereal packet is good for this

Ruler

Pencil

Scissors

Plastic bags in lots of different colors

Felt-tipped pen

Pinking shears (optional)

Stapler

Ribbon (at least 2 yards/meters but as long as you want it)

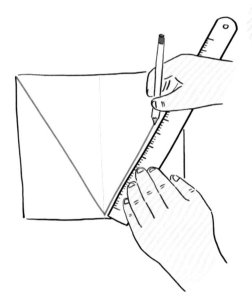

1 On paper, draw a square with sides about 8½ in (21 cm) and cut it out. Fold it in half to find the center. With your ruler draw lines from the center of the bottom edge to the two top corners to make an isosceles triangle. Cut along these lines. Now draw around it onto the card and cut it out again to make a strong template—you will need to use it lots of times.

2 Cut open your plastic bags and open them out. Use your paper or cardstock triangle as a template—draw around it onto plastic bags with a felt-tipped pen. You should be able to get two or even three triangles per bag.

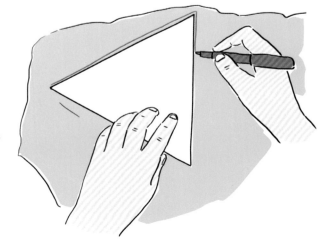

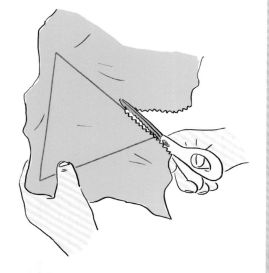

3 Cut out the triangles using pinking shears so that they have a nice patterned edge. Don't worry if you don't have any pinking shears, as ordinary scissors will be fine.

Bring out the BUNTING!

4 Starting about 10 in (26 cm) from the end of the ribbon, begin to staple the triangles onto the ribbon. Use three or four staples for each triangle. You could leave small spaces—1 in (2.5 cm)—between the triangles or have them touching. Leave another 10 in (26 cm) for tying at the other end. Use the ends of the ribbon to tie the bunting in place.

Pine Cone Bird Feeder

Birds might sometimes steal fruit and vegetables you are growing in your garden, but they are your friends because they eat the caterpillars and other bugs that might eat your plants. In the summer and fall (autumn) they can usually find plenty to eat but may need some help in the winter and spring. This pretty feeder is made with pine cones and berries. Hang it near your window and watch the birds feed.

You will need

Paintbrush

Gold or silver acrylic paint

Paint tray or plastic container

2–3 small pine cones

Garden twine or string, 24 in (60 cm) in length

1 large pine cone

Sprays of rowan berries (you could also use hawthorn berries or rosehips—make sure you pick them with long enough stems for tying)

Apron

½ cup (65 g) birdseed

½ cup (65 g) flour

1 cup (125 g) oatmeal

½ cup (115 g) white fat (lard), at room temperature

Mixing bowl

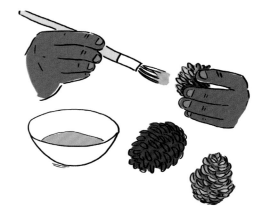

1 Using your paintbrush, dab the gold or silver paint to the scales of the smaller pine cones, and then leave them to dry.

2 Tie one end of the string or twine around the center of the largest pine cone and then tie a small pine cones a bit further up. Making a slip knot is the easiest way to tie it on.

Wind the string once around your fingers and cross the ends. Slide the loop off your fingers, hold it in one hand, and with the other hand push a loop of the long end up through the finger loop.

Take hold of this second loop and, with the other hand, pull the two ends so the first loop tightens around the second one (try to find someone to teach you how to do this).

Put the pine cone through the loop—it will widen if you pull it—and then pull the two ends to tighten it

Safety

Never try eating wild berries or berries from the garden, unless an adult has told you they are safe. Many pretty berries, including rowan berries, are poisonous to humans.

3 A bit further up, tie on a spray of berries. Keep going like this, leaving at least 8 in (20 cm) clear at the end for tying to a branch.

4 This next part is a messy activity so put on an apron! Tip the birdseed, flour, oatmeal, and white fat (lard) into the mixing bowl. Mix everything together using your hands. (You could use a wooden spoon but it's easier and more fun with your hands.)

Tips

Once you start feeding garden birds, keep doing so, as they will come to rely on these snacks. If you want to make decorative feeders in the winter, you could collect a lot of berries and ask a grown-up to freeze them for you. But label them well—you don't want someone to mistake them for human food when they go to the freezer!

5 Push the mixture into the gaps in the large pine cone until it is as full as possible. When you have finished, ask an adult to hang your bird feeder in a tree or somewhere you can easily watch the birds come and visit.

Ice Mobiles

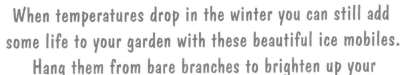

When temperatures drop in the winter you can still add some life to your garden with these beautiful ice mobiles. Hang them from bare branches to brighten up your backyard and, remember, the colder it is, the longer they will last.

You will need

Plain or shaped silicone cupcake molds

Large flat-bottomed plastic container

Selection of fall (autumn) berries, such as sorbus, pyracantha, or cotoneaster

Sparkly glitter

Pretty ribbon

Small pitcher (jug)

1 Place the cupcake molds in a row in the plastic container and add some fall (autumn) berries to each mold.

Tip

You can use other natural treasures from the garden instead of the berries. Why not try freezing some tiny pebbles, seedheads, or leaves with the glitter?

Safety

Never try eating wild berries or berries from the garden, unless an adult has told you they are safe. Many pretty berries are poisonous to humans.

2 Carefully sprinkle a little of the sparkly glitter into each of the molds. Try to get a nice mixture of colors because then the glitter will really catch the light when you hang the mobile outside.

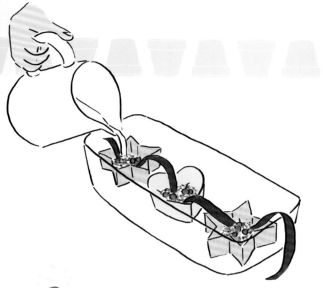

3 Place the length of ribbon across all the molds so that it dangles into each one and there is at least 12 in (30 cm) spare at one end for tying to a branch. Carefully pour water from the pitcher (jug) into each of the molds until they are all full. Make sure that the ribbon hangs right into the water in each of the molds.

ICE JEWELS to catch the sun

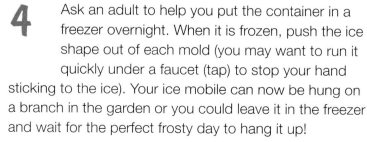

4 Ask an adult to help you put the container in a freezer overnight. When it is frozen, push the ice shape out of each mold (you may want to run it quickly under a faucet (tap) to stop your hand sticking to the ice). Your ice mobile can now be hung on a branch in the garden or you could leave it in the freezer and wait for the perfect frosty day to hang it up!

Mini Scarecrow ●○○

Make a mini scarecrow to keep the birds off your plot by using some of your own old clothes or some from a little brother or sister. If you don't have any dungarees, have a look in local thrift stores or charity shops to see what you can find.

You will need

Thick bamboo cane, approximately 20 in (50 cm) long

Old broomstick

Garden twine or string

Scissors

Small child's dungarees

Long-sleeved child's T-shirt

Old plastic bags, or straw, for stuffing

Small amount of extra straw

Terracotta plant pot, approximately 8 in (20 cm) in diameter

Old straw hat

1 Put the bamboo cane across the broom handle about a third of the way down from the top to form a cross shape. Wrap the garden twine or string several times around the join in a figure-of-eight pattern and then tie it tightly to hold the cross shape together.

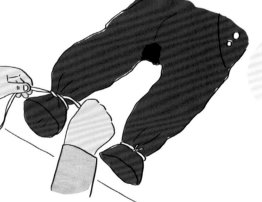

2 Cut a hole big enough for the broomstick between the legs of the dungarees. Then, using the twine or string, tie the ends of the legs closed, but not too tight so you can push in some straw later.

3 Stuff the legs of the dungarees with scrunched-up plastic bags or straw.

4 "Dress" the cross shape poles in the old T-shirt and then thread the pole through the hole you have cut in the dungarees. Pull the dungarees up over the top the T-shirt and button up the straps over the scarecrow's shoulders.

5 Using the twine or string, tie the ends of the sleeves closed around the bamboo cane, but, again, not too tight so you can push in some straw later.

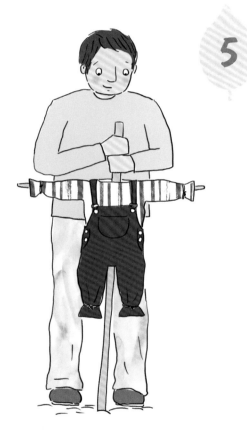

6 Ask an adult to help you push or hammer the base of the long broomstick into the ground in the spot you've chosen, so that the scarecrow stands up securely with it legs dangling a little way above the soil.

7 Now stuff the scarecrow's body and arms with more plastic bags or straw until he or she is nice and plump.

8 Push a little straw into the ends of the sleeves and dungaree legs so it sticks out and looks like hands and feet. Push in more around the top of the T-shirt to look like a neck.

9 Place the plant-pot head on the scarecrow and finish off by adding the hat.

Tip

Why not make scarecrows in different sizes using clothes for babies, toddlers, and children? Just make the length of the broom handles slightly smaller each time.

Bird Scarers

☺ ◯ ◯

Birds are great to watch in the garden and they will also eat the bugs that might eat your plants, but sometimes they can be tempted to gobble up your seeds, fruit, or even young plants. Keep them away from your crops and brighten up your vegetable patch at the same time with this pretty bird scarer.

You will need

4 bamboo canes about 40 in (1 meter) tall

Garden twine or string

Long length of thin ribbon

Old CD

A few plastic milk bottle tops

A pointy pair of scissors and chopping board

Aluminum foil

Short lengths of wider ribbon and sparkly tinsel

1 Take the bamboo canes and push two of them into the ground at either end of your row of crops to form upside-down "V"-shapes.

2 Tie the bamboo canes tightly together at the top using the garden twine or string in a figure-of-eight pattern.

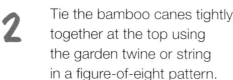

3 Measure off a piece of the thin ribbon so that it is approximately 8 in (20 cm) longer than the gap between the two bamboo-cane supports.

4 Tie one end of the ribbon to the first set of bamboo canes, tying it around the string join at the top of the canes, before threading on the old CD. Tie the other end to the second set of bamboo canes. Remember to ask an adult for permission to use the CD first!

5 Make holes in the plastic bottle tops by carefully pushing and twisting through them with the point of the scissors, into a chopping board (ask an adult to help if you find this difficult).

6 Wrap aluminum foil around each bottle top. Push a hole through the foil on top of the hole through the plastic. Thread each bottle top onto a length of string and knot one end to stop it falling off.

7 Tie short lengths of the wider ribbon, pieces of tinsel, and the strings with the bottle tops on them onto the central ribbon, making sure that you space everything at regular intervals. The fluttering ribbons, shiny tops, and tinsel will scare away any birds.

Tip

Birds will get used to your bird scarer after a few days, so why not change around some of the items on the ribbon? You could try adding strips of aluminum foil or plastic bags—anything that is shiny or moves about will scare away birds.

Shoo, shoo, SHOO!

Painted Pots

Brighten up your garden with these terracotta plant pots, which have been painted in fun colors and decorated with bold contrasting spots. Plant them with your favorite plants and use them indoors or out, or give them as gifts to friends and relatives.

You will need

Terracotta plant pots

Paper plate or plastic container for paints

A medium-sized paintbrush

A fine paintbrush

White undercoat

Paint in assorted colors

Pencil

Water-based acrylic varnish

1 Start by painting your terracotta pots with a layer of undercoat. Turn them upside down and paint all over the outside using a medium-sized paintbrush. When the paint has dried, turn the pot over and paint the inside of the pot with the undercoat to about halfway down, so that the terracotta does not show.

2 Decide what color you want for the main color of your paint and paint the outside and inside of the pot in the same way. Allow it to dry completely. If the color looks a little streaky, paint a second coat and allow to dry.

3 Use a pencil to draw your the spots on the outside of the pot. (If you want your spots to be perfect circles, draw round a coin or circle of cardboard.)

SPOTS on pots!

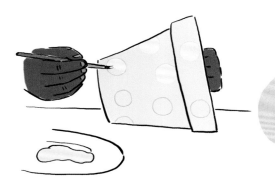

4 Now it is time to fill in your spots! Use a fine paintbrush to paint the spots in a contrasting color. Allow to dry.

Tips

• Broad stripes in contrasting colors also look great painted around pots. Once you have applied the base color, use a pencil and draw them on the pot.

• Terracotta flowerpot saucers can be painted to match the pots.

• Use a fine brush to paint vegetable motifs on the pots—red tomatoes, chunky orange carrots, or green beans would all look great!

5 Finish the pot with a coat of water-based acrylic varnish over the paint.

chapter 4
Garden Crafts

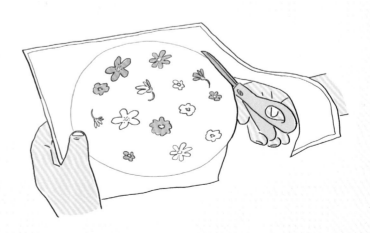

Crystallized Pansies

Real flowers make the prettiest of decorations for cupcakes, and they taste good too. Egg white and superfine (caster) sugar is all you need to create these pretty crystallized flowers.

You will need

2 eggs

2 plates

Egg cup

Bowl

Teaspoon

Egg whisk

Fine paintbrush

Fresh pansies

Superfine (caster) sugar

Cupcakes

Cake plate or cake stand

1 First separate the egg whites from the egg yolks. Firmly tap an egg on the side of a plate and then pull the two halves apart with your fingertips—make sure you keep the yolk whole! Put an egg cup over the yolk and, holding the plate over a bowl, tip the plate so that the egg white slides into the bowl. Repeat with the other egg. Add one teaspoon of water to the egg whites and then beat them with an egg whisk until they are frothy.

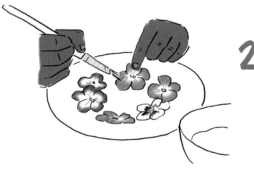

2 Using a fine paintbrush, carefully paint each flower with egg white. Paint no more than seven or eight flowers at a time, as the egg white dries quite quickly. Lay each one on a plate as you finish it.

3 Use a spoon to sprinkle superfine (caster) sugar over the flowers, making sure not to add too much sugar. Leave to dry overnight or longer. The flowers will become hard and brittle.

Hints and Tips

• There are many edible flowers, including roses and nasturtiums—make sure you check which ones you can eat.

• Pick the flowers on a dry day—if they are damp, they will go mushy.

• Pregnant women, elderly people, and very young children should avoid eating raw egg white.

EDIBLE flowers!

4 Use three or four of the flowers to decorate each cupcake. Serve on a pretty cake plate or glass cake stand.

Pressed Flower Placemats ●●○○

Pressing flowers is a clever way of making sure that they don't fade and die but will last for ever. Once you have pressed them, make them into pretty placemats so that everyone can enjoy them all year round. You could even press flowers at different times of the year to create a range of placemats for every season.

You will need

Small garden flowers

Heavy books

Sheets of newspaper

Sheets of letter size (A4) paper

Large plate

Pencil

Sheets of ledger size (A3) thick white cardstock—one for each mat

Sharp scissors

Contact paper or clear sticky-backed plastic

White (PVA) glue

1 Pick some small flowers from your favorite garden plants, remembering to ask an adult for permission first.

2 Find a place in your room which won't be disturbed and gather the books together. Place one book flat with a folded sheet of newspaper on top. Lay a sheet of plain paper on top of the newspaper and then arrange some flowers on this so that they don't touch each other. Place another piece of plain paper on top and then some more newspaper. If you have more flowers to press, put down another piece of plain paper and build up the layers in the same way as before. Finally pile on some heavy books. Now leave them undisturbed for at least two weeks to fully dry out.

3 When the flowers are dry, draw around the large plate with the pencil to make a circle on the piece of thick card. Cut a square of contact paper or sticky-backed plastic that is just bigger than the circle.

Tip

You can make matching coasters by drawing around a large mug or small bowl to create a smaller circle.

4 Arrange the flowers on your card circle and, when you are happy with the pattern, stick them on carefully by putting a small dab of white (PVA) glue onto the back of each flower.

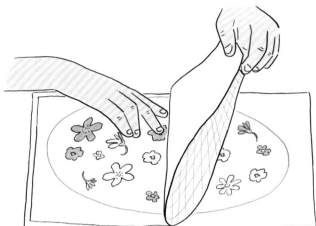

5 When your pattern is finished and the glue has dried, peel away the backing from one edge of the contact paper, position it carefully over the circle of flowers, and press down. Then, start to peel away the rest of the backing, smoothing down the contact paper as you go. Try hard not to wrinkle it or trap any air bubbles. (This part is quite tricky and you may need to ask an adult to help you.)

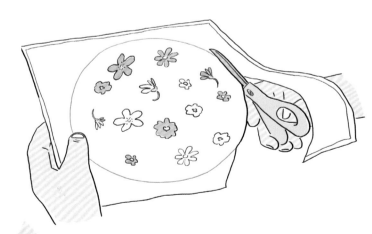

6 Now cut carefully around the edge of the circle, cutting through the plastic and the cardboard. You can make more mats in the same way until you have a set.

Pretty Seed Packets

It is fun and satisfying to harvest your own seeds. Seeds come in all shapes and sizes and so do the seed heads. Look for pepper-pot poppy heads and shake the seeds out of these or take shiny pink and black cranberry (borlotti) beans from their pods. Once you have harvested the seeds, package them for the following year in pretty decorated envelopes that you have designed yourself. They make great presents for family and friends.

You will need

Scissors

Paper bags

Small brown envelopes

Colored pencils

Hole punch

White plate

Raffia ribbon—about 10 in (25 cm) per packet

1 At the end of summer, when the seed heads are drying on the plants, begin to collect your seeds. Harvest them from any plant which attracts bees or other insects. Harvest in the afternoon, when the weather is dry, but only when the seed heads have turned brown or yellow and look dried out.

2 Cut the seed heads off and put them in a paper bag. Use a different bag for each type of plant and don't forget to label which is which! Give the bag a good shake so that the seeds fall out of the seed heads, and open tough pods, then leave the bags in a dry, airy place to completely dry for a few days.

3 When the seeds are ready, decorate your envelopes. Decorate the edges of the front of the envelope with pretty designs such as wavy lines and tiny polka dots.

4 Now draw the shape of a flower or vegetable, depending on what seeds you have collected, and fill in the design using the colored pencils. You may like to add the name of the seeds in your best handwriting.

5 Close, but don't seal, the flap of the envelope, then use a hole punch to make two holes through the envelope and the flap, at the top of the envelope.

6 Now, one bag at a time, tip the seeds you have collected onto a white plate. Separate the seeds from bits of seed casing, small insects that have crept inside, and anything else which isn't a seed! Carefully put the seeds into the correct envelope, and seal it closed.

7 Thread the raffia through the two punched holes and tie in a decorative bow. Trim the ends of the raffia with scissors to finish.

Hints and Tips

• Wrap tiny seeds in a piece of tissue paper and seal with tape before placing in the envelope.

• These envelopes would also look great decorated with vegetable-print designs—see pages 104–105.

• Make yourself sound professional—look up on the internet the Latin names for the plants and write them on the front in your very best handwriting!

Seeds for friends in pretty PACKETS

Herbal Bath Bag

Herbs from the garden needn't just be for eating. You can use them, instead, to make scented herbal bath bags. When you're freezing after a tough sports match or when you've been camping in the rain, tie one over the hot faucet (tap) and lie back for a super-scented soak in the tub. You can use fresh herbs or dry herbs for these.

You will need

Large dinner plate

Pencil

Piece of muslin

Pinking shears

Fresh or dried herbs, such as lavender, sage, rosemary, thyme, mint, and bay leaves

Rubber band

Pretty ribbons

1 Take the plate and draw around it with the pencil on the piece of muslin. Cut out the circle of muslin with the pinking shears. Using pinking shears will stop the fabric from fraying at the edges.

2 Put your chosen herbs in the middle of the circle of muslin. If you are going to use the bath bags straight away, use sprigs of fresh herbs. If you want to keep them for longer, then use dried herbs.

Tip

You can dry herbs for your bath bags by hanging them upside down for a few weeks in small bunches somewhere warm and dry.

3 Gather together the fabric and twist it around so that the herbs are contained in the center of the piece of muslin. Use a rubber band to secure the fabric tightly.

SUPER-SCENTED bathtime!

4 Take one of the ribbons and tie it carefully over the rubber band so that the band is hidden from view. Tie a double knot so that it won't come loose and then you can tie the ribbon into a bow on top in order to finish it off.

5 Slip another length of ribbon under the first ribbon and the rubber band, and tie this on with a knot. Use this section of ribbon to secure your bath bag to the hot faucet (tap) at bath-time but be careful— ask an adult to help if the faucet (tap) is very hot.

Printed Apron

A gardening apron is really useful to keep you clean and to hold some tools. Make yours special with a printed design of apples, printed with real apples. You can use a ready-bought apron or, if you like sewing, you can make your own from cream calico and colorful bias binding.

You will need

Apple

Sharp knife for cutting the apple

Chopping board

Paper towel

Fabric paint

Large flat plate

Small sponge paint roller

Scrap paper

Plain cotton apron

Iron

Hints and Tips

• Try cutting different fruits and vegetables, such as broccoli, carrots, and cauliflower, in half—they will all create interesting veggie motifs on fabric.

• This traditional printing method is fun and easy, and works just as well on cards and paper as on fabric.

1 Use a sharp knife to cut the apple in half. Remember to cut down on a chopping board and hold the apple with your hand in a bridge shape, so the knife is clear of your fingers. Blot the cut sides of the apple with paper towel to remove any moisture.

2 Squirt some paint onto a plate, and roll the roller through it, spreading out the paint. Scrape off any excess paint on the side of plate. Roll the roller over the flat surface of the apple so that it is completely covered in paint. Experiment by printing on a piece of paper before you print on your apron. When you are ready, roll some more paint onto your apple.

3 Carefully place the apple cut-side down on the apron and press down firmly to make the print. Use a slight rocking motion to make sure that the paint on every bit of the cut apple has touched the apron, but be careful not slide the apple as this will smudge the print.

4 Using the roller, apply more paint to the apple, then repeat the design all the way around the apron, as many times as you like. Allow the paint to dry thoroughly.

5 When the paint is completely dry, ask an adult to help you iron the apron to seal the paint (following the manufacturer's instructions). You will then be able to get your apron dirty in the garden and wash it afterward without worrying about the apple design washing off.

Print... print... print... PRINT

Painted Stones

Look for pebbles and stones in the shape of houses—you need something with a flat bottom and a rounded top—and paint them to look like cute cottages. But don't let your imagination stop there—you can paint almost anything you like, such as faces, animals, or garden creepy-crawlies.

You will need

Stones in various sizes with a flattish bottom

Medium paintbrushes

Paints

Fine paintbrushes

White (PVA) glue

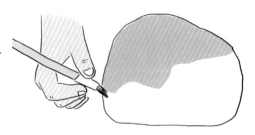

1 Use a medium paintbrush to paint the bottom half of a large stone with white paint for the walls of the house. Leave to dry. Then, if you can still see the stone through the paint, cover it again with another coat.

2 When the white paint is completely dry, paint the roof using a darker color—orange or brown are good colors for a roof although you can use any other you particularly like. Leave to dry.

3 Use a fine paintbrush to paint a door and windows onto the stone using a variety of colors.

paint a pretty COTTAGE

4 Now you can add lots of pretty details! Paint tiles onto the roof or add some criss-cross lines to make it look like a thatched roof. Add flowers in window boxes and growing by the door and add vines or climbing plants around the door.

5 When the paint is completely dry, mix some white (PVA) glue with a little water to dilute it and use it to paint over all of the stone. This will make it nice and shiny and will also protect your painted house from bumps and scratches.

Pumpkin Animals

There's no need to stop at carving pumpkins when it comes to Halloween. Experiment by making all sorts of creatures from pumpkins, squash, and other vegetables to add fun to your Halloween party, and when you have finished you can still cook and eat everything you have used! Squash are like pumpkins, so if you want to grow your own see pages 72–75.

You will need

Pumpkins and squash in any shape, size, and color

Selection of other vegetables— carrots, Brussels sprouts, eggplants (aubergine), and zucchini (courgette) are all great

Pumpkin and sunflower seeds, fresh ginger root, bay leaves

Sharp knife

Chopping board

Toothpicks (cocktail sticks)

Wooden skewers

1 Lay all your vegetables out on the table so that you can see what you have got. Start thinking about which animals you would like to make and play around with different arrangements to create some crazy creatures!

2 Push one end of a toothpick (cocktail stick) into the vegetable you would like to use, such as a carrot, and then push the other end into your pumpkin.

3 Push seeds into pumpkins to make eyebrows, teeth, nose, etc.

4 Seeds make great spikes for hedgehogs. Push them into a squash, using the pointed top of the squash as a nose.

Let your imagination go WILD!

5 Use a sharp knife and chopping board to cut slices of vegetables. (Remember to keep your fingers out of the way or ask an adult to help you.) The slices make great eyes when held in place with toothpicks.

6 Push half of one of the wooden skewers into a squash to join one onto the other. Ask an adult to help if the skin of the squash is very tough.

7   Push another squash onto the rest of the skewer to join two together.

8   Make antlers, ears, arms, and eyes by attaching them to the squash with toothpicks —Brussels sprouts make great ears!

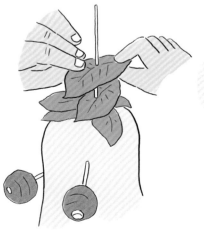

9   Bay leaves are a good shape to use as hair or headdresses and decoration on your creatures. It is easy to push toothpicks through them, which can then be pushed into the pumpkins.

Suppliers and Resources

Your local garden center will probably have all the things you need to get going in the garden but here are some useful websites for places that sell children's tools and gardening and craft materials.

US

Arizona Pottery
www.arizonapottery.com
Good selection of pots and planters for indoor and outdoor use.

Avant Gardens
www.avantgardensne.com
Garden nursery selling a wide selection of plants online.

Backyard Gardener
www.backyardgardener.com
A good source of information as well as selling a wide range of vegetable seeds.

Gardener's Supply Company
www.gardeners.com
Tools, pots and containers, seeds, plants, and more.

Hobby Lobby
www.hobbylobby.com
Stores nationwide.

Irish Eyes Garden Seeds
www.irisheyesgardenseeds.com
Offers a large selection of organic vegetable seeds and potato tubers.

Kids Gardening
www.kidsgardening.org
Part of The National Gardening Association, with lots of information and resources.

Michaels
www.michaels.com
Stores nationwide.

Nichols Garden Nursery
www.nicholsgardennursery.com
Every kind of vegetable seed imaginable, as well as herb plants, strawberry plants, and gardening supplies and tools.

UK

Baker Ross
www.bakerross.co.uk
Huge range of craft supplies.

B&Q
www.diy.com
Wide selection of terracotta plant pots and saucers, plus plants and seeds and gardening tools.

Capital Gardens
www.capitalgardens.co.uk
Great selection of plants and seeds, plus a variety of kid-sized tools, gloves, rain capes, boots, and garden baskets and trugs. Also stones, pebbles, and pots.

Dan the Gardener
www.danthegardener.co.uk
Useful gardening advice for kids plus colorful, good-quality kids' garden tools.

Harrod Horticultural
www.harrodhorticultural.com
High-quality stainless-steel kids' tools that look just like the grown-up versions. Also boots, aprons, and gloves.

Hobbycraft
www.hobbycraft.co.uk
Chain of craft superstores carrying everything the young garden crafter needs.

Homebase
www.homebase.co.uk
DIY stores with a garden section selling annuals and other plants, as well as terracotta pots, bowls and saucers, garden tools, and polished pebbles.

Jekka's Herb Farm
www.jekkasherbfarm.com
A specialist all-organic herb nursery.

John Lewis
www.johnlewis.co.uk
A good seasonal selection of tools, watering cans and seeds for budding young gardeners.

Mr Fothergills
www.mr-fothergills.co.uk
Huge selection of flower and vegetable seeds.

Parkers
www.jparkers.co.uk
Good value source of mail-order bulbs.

Spear & Jackson
www.spear-and-jackson.com/products/garden-tools/childrens
Suppliers of proper gardening tools for children.

Spotty Green Frog
www.spottygreenfrog.co.uk
Educational play website with a useful section on Outdoor Play where you can find proper gardening tools for children.

Suttons Seeds
www.suttons.co.uk
A special selection of child-friendly seeds that are easy to grow.

Thompson & Morgan
www.thompson-morgan.com
Potato tubers and a large selection of flower and vegetable seeds.

Index

Credits

Key: t = top, c = center,
b = bottom, l = left, r = right

Project makers
Susan Akass: pp 72–75
Emma Hardy: pp 35–37, 38–40,
41–43, 50–51, 54–55, 78–79,
106–107, 108–110
Dawn Isaac: pp 47–49, 52–53,
60–62, 66–68, 69–71, 80–81,
82–83, 84–86, 87–89, 96–98,
102–103
Catherine Woram/Martyn Cox:
pp 30–31, 32–34, 44–46,
56–59, 63–65, 90–91, 94–95,
99–101, 104–105

Photography
Kim Lightbody: p 9t
Emma Mitchell: pp 1, 2, 4, 6, 7, 8,
9b, 23, 27t, 27b, 29r, 49, 53, 61,
62, 67, 71, 76, 77b, 81, 83, 85,
86, 87, 89, 93c, 97, 98, 103
Debbie Patterson: pp 28, 37, 39,
43, 51, 55, 77t, 79, 93b, 107,
109, 110
Hervé Ronciere: pp 26, 73, 75
Polly Wreford: pp 3, 11, 12, 21, 29l,
31, 33, 45, 57, 65, 77l, 91, 92,
93t, 95, 99, 101, 105